# A Mississippi
## *Spring*
## on Bluebird Hill

A true story about our little
farm in the hills of Southern Mississippi

ISBN: 1-59571-004-3
Library of Congress Control Number: 2004107386


**Hot Chocolate Books**
a division of Word Association Publishers
205 Fifth Avenue
Tarentum, Pennsylvania 15084
www.wordassociation.com

# A Mississippi *Spring* on Bluebird Hill

A true story about our little
farm in the hills of Southern Mississippi

by
Billie Remson

Hot Chocolate
BOOKS

A Division of

Word Association Publishers
205 Fifth Avenue
Tarentum, Pennsylvania 15084

Written for children and adults who would like to know
what life is like living on a farm for the fun of it.  And for
those who just enjoy remembering.

To my loving husband, Marcel
who has given me my heart's desire— a farmhouse
on a hill overlooking a pond, and a Shetland
sheepdog at my side

*"There is a time for everything*
*and a season for every activity."* Ecclesiastes 3:1a
Holy Bible: New International Version, Holman Bible Publishers, Colorado Springs, CO

# *Spring*

Mama B and Papa Doc live in a pretty little farmhouse in the rolling hills of southern Mississippi. The front yard leading down the hill from their farmhouse slopes gently toward a dam that has created a beautiful lake. The pine trees, on the far side of the lake, form a background of deep green. A white egret walks slowly around the edge of the lake and just as quick as a flash his head goes into the water. He has caught a small fish for his dinner. The egret holds his head back and swallows the fish whole, then resumes his slow walk, waiting for the next course of his meal.

Mama B and Papa Doc are sitting on the back porch where they see a nosy squirrel in the big oak tree nearby. He is their first animal friend to come to the farm. He is trying to communicate using sounds because he knows he

1

is being watched. He shows off by hanging onto a tree limb with his back feet. Then he sits up on the limb and flicks his tail a few times and jumps to a higher limb. This squirrel is unusual because he has white ears and a black-and-white face. Papa Doc said, "An unusual squirrel needs an unusual name, so let's name our new friend Fritz."

Mama B and Papa Doc are very happy that Fritz has come out of the woods to join their farm family and to live in the big oak tree near the house. He is good company.

Mama B and Papa Doc continue to rock in their rocking chairs as they watch Eastern bluebirds flying around in the yard looking for a place to build a nest. Papa Doc says, "Let's name our little farm Bluebird Hill since Eastern bluebirds live in this area of the south all year."

Mama B is happy with the name Papa Doc has chosen. They have been trying for several months to decide on the perfect name for their farm.

Bluebird Hill is located in the gentle hills of south-central Mississippi, five miles from the nearest town. It is actually nestled between the towns of Tylertown and McComb. Walthall County, where Tylertown is located, is home to many fine cows and is proudly known as "the cream pitcher of Mississippi." Mama B and Papa Doc look forward to the annual dairy festival the county holds each June. The delicious homemade ice cream is a special treat they enjoy.

The town of McComb, in Pike County, Mississippi, is a showplace in the spring when the beautiful flowering azalea shrubs are in full bloom. Mama B and Papa Doc always mark their calendar to remember the days in March when the town shows off its beauty with the Azalea Festival Tour and the Lighted Azalea Trail.

The Bogue Chitto River Water Park, only three miles from Bluebird Hill, is a great place to cool off during Mississippi's warm spring and hot summer months. People in canoes and tubes drift down the winding, lazy river that snakes through the valley. Inviting, snow-white sandbars along the way are perfect for resting or playing in the sand. If you come visit, it's not at all unusual to catch a glimpse of Mama B and Papa Doc lounging on a sandbar enjoying Mama B's special, delicious sugar cookies and some lemonade. On particularly warm days, you'll likely see them in their canoe, floating along on the cool currents.

The state line of Louisiana is only ten miles to the south of Bluebird Hill. When you cross into Louisiana, the land levels out to the flatlands of the coastal areas and the great Gulf of Mexico. The big city of New Orleans is located exactly eighty-five miles south of Bluebird Hill.

Many people from New Orleans like to vacation in the quiet, pine-tree hills of southern Mississippi near Bluebird Hill. In turn, local people from Mississippi like to travel to New Orleans for a taste of big-city life. It works out just fine for Mama B and Papa Doc because they love meeting and greeting the visitors from the big city just as much as they enjoy their occasional trips to New Orleans to shop and dine in the world-famous restaurants of the magical Crescent City.

In fact, folks who live near Bluebird Hill, along with people all the way to New Orleans, are proud of their region's interesting combination of home cooking and spicy Cajun food. They all think that Louisiana and Mississippi "potluck" dinners are just grand. Why, at any one of them, you might chow down something as homespun as chicken 'n dumplins or as exotic as jambalaya, which is a mixture of chicken, shrimp, oysters, ham, rice, and sausage—a fascinating combination just like all of us.

As the sun begins to warm the cold ground at the beginning of March, the plants of spring start popping out of the earth. The white narcissus and yellow daffodils that were planted in the autumn as bulbs are the first flowers to make an appearance. The fruit trees on the hillside are covered in white and pink flowers. In the woods nearby, the dogwood and redbud trees are in full bloom. The oak trees have started budding and blades of green grass can be seen  sprouting near the house. The birds are singing to welcome springtime on Bluebird Hill.

In some areas of the northern states snow is still on the ground and children are playing all bundled up as the snow plows clear the roads. Smoke from the chimneys can be seen over the countryside as  these cold days of winter continue in the north.

The birds are migrating back from South America and the southern most coastal regions of the United States where they spent their winter in a warmer climate. Some of the birds make Bluebird Hill a rest  stop since Mama B has made sure the feeders are full. They will stay in the warmer climate of Mississippi for awhile, resting and getting their strength back. When the snow melts in the North, they will continue their journey to spend their summer in places like New York, Minnesota, and Pennsylvania.

Papa Doc has built fifteen bluebird houses and placed them on fence posts in the yard. He has spaced them out because bluebirds like to have their own territory.

One day when Papa Doc was putting a birdhouse on a post, a bluebird perched atop a nearby pine tree and watched, cocking his head this way and that. It was as if he were trying to tell Papa Doc, "That house is for me!" The bright blue male bluebird was apparently scouting for a place for a nest. The male bluebird selects several places to nest and then shows the sites to the female. It is the female who decides where the nest will be built. Together they bring twigs to the site, but the female does the actual building. She uses twigs and lines the nest with soft grass clippings and leaves.

Mama B is happy with all these pretty birds to watch and spring flowers to enjoy, but she tells Papa Doc, "There are still some things we need, like a barn, a tractor, and farm animals, to make Bluebird Hill a real farm."

During the warm days of spring Papa Doc starts to build the barn. He has decided that the barn must have a tin roof so that he can hear the pitter-patter of the spring raindrops as they hit the metal. Papa Doc is going to paint the barn green so that it blends in with the pine trees that grow behind it.

Papa Doc also needs to buy a tractor and a disc to break the ground for planting. He will use the disc when he prepares the spring vegetable garden and plants food plots for the animals. He will also need to buy a rotary mower for the weeds and grass, and a scoop and a box grader to move dirt from place to place. All of these tools will keep Papa Doc busy and very happy.

The first farm animal, Mama B and Papa Doc decide, will have to be a dog. Mama B has wished for a collie dog since she was a little girl. While reading the "pets for sale" section of the local newspaper, Mama B spies an ad for Shetland sheepdog puppies who need homes. A Shetland sheepdog looks like a little collie. That's close enough for Mama B.

Papa Doc is on the tractor, mowing the grass with the rotary mower. Mama B runs out of the farmhouse toward the tractor shouting, "Turn off that tractor! I have news!"

In the sudden silence, she announces, "I am going to look at some puppies and I am probably going to bring one home."

Papa Doc looks at Mama B with his twinklie,
little, brown beaded eyes and just nods his head
yes. He knows Mama B is going to do just as she
says, no matter what *he* says. Anything that
makes Mama B happy makes Papa Doc happy.
So Papa Doc cranks the tractor back to life and
continues his work mowing the yard as Mama B
drives off in the pickup truck.

There are two puppies who need a home. One runs under the house while the other comes to sit on Mama B's foot. One look at the six-week-old puppy sitting on her foot reminds Mama B of the collie she has always wanted. It is instant "puppy love" for Mama B. This puppy is a keeper.

The puppy rides in Mama B's lap all the way home to Bluebird Hill while Mama B tries to think of the perfect name for him. The puppy struggles to lick her face. He knows he has found someone who will love him and Mama B knows she has chosen the right puppy.

When Mama B arrives back at Bluebird Hill, she is so excited she can hardly wait to show Papa Doc the puppy. Papa Doc sees Mama B coming down the gravel road in the pick-up truck and stops the tractor. He knows she has a puppy by the way she is waving her arm out the window and honking the horn.

Kym Garraway...

Kym Garraway...

Kym Garraway

Kym
Garraway...

Mama B gets out of the pick-up truck with the puppy cuddled close to her body. The six-week-old puppy looks like a ball of tan fuzz. He has a long nose, perked-up ears, and round, black eyes. To complete his coat of tan fuzz, he has white fur around his neck and white "socks" on his feet. Papa Doc takes a good look at the pretty little puppy and says with a big smile on his face, "He looks like a Bo to me." Mama B isn't sure about calling him Bo until she gives him the more official sounding name, Beauregard, Mama B's Pride, and then agrees, "But we'll call him Bo."

When Papa Doc finishes mowing the grass with the tractor, he takes the rotary mower off the back of the tractor and puts on the disc. It is time to break up the ground and prepare the vegetable garden for spring planting. Mama B goes into Tylertown to the farm supply store where she buys tomato, cucumber and bell pepper plants. Papa Doc also wants okra, field peas, string bean, and green lima bean seeds. Once the rows are ready for planting, Mama B and Papa Doc plant the vegetable plants and sow the seeds.

A lot of work has to be done during spring to make certain that the vegetable plants and seeds produce. The garden will need to be weeded, watered, plowed, hoed, and fertilized on a regular basis in order to have fresh vegetables during the hot Mississippi summer months ahead.

Chickens! Yes, chickens will be our next addition to the farm. All farmers need a rooster to wake them up in the morning and fresh eggs from the hens to eat for breakfast. And of course to make Mama B's special, delicious sugar cookies. Besides, chickens make great farm pets and are fun to watch.

A friendly neighbor told Papa Doc he would be happy to share his chickens, and he did. He was kind enough to give Papa Doc and Mama B a male bantam chicken, called a rooster, and two little female bantam chickens, called hens. Mama B named the rooster Rufus and the little hens Goldie and Cream.

Bantam chickens are smaller in size than regular chickens and very colorful, especially the roosters. The hens are good layers. They like to nest and hatch baby chicks, called biddies, from the eggs. Chickens lay more eggs in the springtime, and the warm weather is the perfect time to hatch biddies from their eggs.

Papa Doc wants the chickens to have a special chicken house on Bluebird Hill, so he gets his hammer and goes to work building a chicken house, complete with a window and door. He cuts a small hole in the bottom of the door so the chickens can go outside into the yard.

When the chickens take their first stroll in the yard, Mama B and Bo are there to watch.

The puppy Bo has never seen a chicken before and the chickens have never seen a dog. So when Goldie and Cream get their first glimpse of Bo, the feathers really begin to fly! Bo, of course, thinks the squawking and running is a great game, so he joins in the chase, trying his best to catch the little hens.

Horrified, Mama B runs right behind Bo and tries to stop him. The chickens, Mama B and Bo go around and around the yard until Mama B finally catches Bo. She takes him into the barn where she gives him a light but loving swat with a newspaper and a very serious scolding. Bo won't be chasing the chickens again. He'll learn to be their friend and protector.

Papa Doc has decided that chickens need furniture just like people, only a different kind. They need a roost and nest built inside their house. They also need a "chicken walk" so that

they can get on the roost.

    With Bo by his side, Papa Doc goes into the woods and cuts six branches from trees to use as poles for the roost and the chicken walk.    He nails five poles across the inside of the chicken house, wall to wall, so the chickens will  have a roost to get on at night.  He uses the last pole to make a chicken walk by nailing small strips of wood across the pole, spacing the boards about twelve inches apart.  He nails the chicken walk to the highest roost pole and rests the bottom of the pole on the ground.  Now the chickens can use the chicken walk as a ladder to get on their roost.

Late in the afternoon, Goldie and Cream jump on the lowest roost pole and then hop from one roost pole to the next until they reach the highest pole where they roost. When they are on the roost at night, they are sleeping.  There they feel safe from rats, weasels,  or other critters that may harm them.  The chickens sleep until Rufus wakes them up with his loud crow at daybreak. With the wake-up call from Rufus, the chickens fly off the roost, ready to  eat and have another fun day on the farm.

Goldie, Cream, and Rufus will have a surprise today. Papa Doc is fencing in the chicken yard. He is putting fence posts in the ground and attaching wire fencing to the posts. The wire is called "chicken wire." The chicken yard is eight feet wide and twenty feet long. When the chickens come out of their little house, they go right into their yard. Wire is placed on top of the fence to keep the chickens from flying out of the yard and also to keep them safe from owls, hawks or other animals that may harm them. The yard has a special gate so that Mama B can go in and out to take care of the chickens.

Now Mama B is bringing sand, a bucket at a time, to make a sand pile for the chickens to dust in. Dusting is when a chicken lays on its side in the sand with its wing stretched out, rolling and scratching in the sand. The sand covers their feathers and skin. This is nature's way for chickens to prevent or get rid of "mites" that sometimes get on them.

The chickens also like to scratch and eat the

granules of sand. The sand helps them to digest their food. Mama B feeds the chickens laying mash, chicken scratch (a mixture of cracked corn and seeds), and crushed oyster shells. When the hens eat crushed oyster shells, their eggs have a thicker shell. Eggs with thicker shells are harder to break. A thick shell also protects the inside of an egg during hot and cold weather.

Goldie and Cream cluck and Rufus crows in appreciation of their new fenced-in yard. They're happy chickens.

Papa Doc loves happy chickens, so now he has decided to build them wooden boxes to be used as nests. He nails the boxes to the inside wall of the chicken house. Mama B rakes pine straw from under the pine trees near the chicken house and places some of it in each nest. Now the hens will have a soft place to lay their eggs. Mama B places a nest egg in each nest. This is a fake or a marked egg that stays in the nest all the time and reminds the little hen where she is to lay her egg. When Mama B gathers the eggs, she always leaves the nest egg in the nest.

The floor of the chicken house is dirt. The chickens like to have pine straw, wood chips, or grass clippings scattered on the dirt floor so that they can scratch and look for bugs. This is the chickens' rug and helps to keep the chicken house clean. Mama B rakes up a big basket of pine straw from the pine trees and scatters it on the floor in the chicken house.

As the lovely Mississippi spring continues, Rufus calls out with a loud squawk to remind Goldie and Cream they need to lay eggs and sit on them so they can have some little baby chicks, called biddies, to call their own. Each hen will lay one egg a day until she has just enough to fit under her little body, so that she can keep each one of them warm.

Every day after laying an egg, Goldie and Cream start to cackle while still on the nest. They cackle for a few minutes, then fly off the nest.  A cackle is the  sound a hen makes to notify the other chickens she  has laid an egg. The rooster, as well as other hens in a chicken house, will cackle with her in celebration of the egg she laid.

When there are several eggs in the nest and a hen wants to set, she will start to cluck. This sound tells the other chickens, and Mama B too, that the hen is  ready to set on the eggs in the nest in order to bring her little biddies into the world.

It takes twenty-one days of setting for eggs to hatch.  During that time, a hen will get off the nest for a few minutes when she needs to take a little walk, eat, or drink water.  While a hen is off the nest, she will cluck and spread her wings to practice what she  will be doing when her baby chicks hatch. But our little mother hens don't stay off their nests very long.  They know that their eggs need the heat from their bodies in order to stay at the correct temperature for them to hatch.

After twenty-one days the baby chicken inside the egg will break the egg shell from the inside with its beak. This tiny break in the egg shell is called a pip. After a pip is made, the egg will start to crack open  and out comes a tiny baby chicken!  The chick is wet when it first hatches but soon dries and becomes a tiny fluffy biddy. Biddies are so small you can hold several of them in the palm of your hand.

While Goldie and Cream sit on their nests keeping their eggs warm, the snow in the northern states is beginning to melt. The geese and ducks sense the change and start their migration back to their summer homes up north. The musical sound of the honking geese can be heard in the distance as they fly over the hills and valleys of Bluebird Hill. They are flying north in a "V" formation, in long lines, and can be recognized easily as they pass overhead.  They seem to be saying, "We will see you in the autumn when we fly south for the winter!"

At last the big day arrives! Goldie and Cream's new babies have hatched and both little hens are clucking with joy over the arrival of all their biddies. Rufus is strutting around as the proud father.

Now the two little mother hens will be kept busy scratching in the sand and grass to find food for their biddies. The hens cluck and the biddies stay close by. If the biddies wander off, a few clucks from the mother hen bring them right back. A cluck is the special sound a hen makes to call her biddies.

A chicken's favorite foods are worms, crickets, and tiny bugs. They also like to eat tender green grass. The hen will scratch in the dirt and find a delicious bug. Then she will cluck and all the biddies will come running. When one lucky biddy gets a bug, it runs with the creature

in its mouth and all the others run after trying to take the bug away. But the little biddy usually swallows the bug before being caught.

Mama B feeds the biddies chicken starter, a special food bought at the farm supply store. It has vitamins to help them grow. Their water container is filled with fresh water every day. Mama B and Papa Doc love to watch as each biddy puts his little beak in the water and holds his head way back to swallow. Rufus stays close to protect the biddies and can't help but crow with joy and pride over his new family.

Because the biddies are too little to get up on the roost at night, the mother hen scratches the straw on the chicken house floor to make a nest to cuddle her little ones. She gathers them under her wings where they are safe and warm at night. Besides, Rufus is just above their heads on the roost and he will warn them if they are in danger.

The biddies are two weeks old now and the little hens have decided that it is time for them to roost. Late in the afternoon Goldie and Cream go into the chicken house. The biddies follow close behind the little hens. Goldie and Cream jump from pole to pole to the highest pole. The biddies look up and see them. They start trying to fly up to their mothers, missing the lowest pole every time. But still, they try and they try.

Mama B and Papa Doc are peeking through the window of the chicken house. They want to help, but know the biddies need to learn how to climb on the roost themselves. The biddies have no idea that Mama B and Papa Doc are watching and enjoying every minute of this learning experience.

At last, the biddies realize there must be an easier way to get on the roost. They discover the chicken walk. Soon they are up on the top pole after a few jumps from board to board on the chicken walk. Now the biddies will sleep on the roost, under Goldie and Cream's wings, until Rufus announces the new day.

Rufus crows so loudly he does a great job waking Mama B and Papa Doc in the farmhouse nearby. He reminds them to "rise and shine" on this sunny spring day. There is work to be done on Bluebird Hill.

Mama B and Papa Doc have a smile on their faces as they sit and swing on the porch, drinking their morning cup of coffee. Bo likes to swing, too and has jumped up to sit with them.

They are planning their workday as they listen to the songs of the birds perched on a limb of the big oak tree in the yard.

Here comes Fritz the squirrel, carrying twigs in his mouth to build a nest in the top of the big oak tree. Mama B and Papa Doc realize they have been so busy with Bo and the chickens that they have been neglecting their little squirrel friend. But Fritz is there to remind them that this is his home, too. As he jumps from limb to limb and hangs by his back feet, he seems to be saying, "Look at me, see what I can do. I am your unusual squirrel with the unusual name, watch me!"

Fritz stops on the limb and sits up. He flicks his tail at the birds. This is his way of telling them that this oak tree belongs to him. However, the birds ignore him and simply continue their morning song.

The end of the Mississippi spring season is almost here. June brings warmer weather in preparation for the hot summer months of July and August. Papa Doc looks at Mama B with his little brown beaded eyes and says, "We gotta get busy. There is work to be done on Bluebird Hill to get ready for summer."

Bo's ears perk up and he leads the way to the barn where Mama B gets her garden tools. Bo starts sniffing and following the trail of a mouse as Papa Doc gets on the tractor. They are happy as they work preparing for summer which will bring new adventures and new friends to Bluebird Hill.

*The End (for now)*

A Bluebird Hill Recipe
***Always ask a grown-up for permission and help BEFORE you begin baking.***

## *Mama B's Special Delicious Sugar Cookies*

1/2 Cup Shortening
1/2 Cup Sugar
1 Egg
1 Cup Self-Rising Flour
1/2 Teaspoon Vanilla Extract

**<u>Ask a grown-up</u> to preheat the oven to 350 degrees before you mix the ingredients together.**

Spray the cookie sheet with cooking spray.

Mix shortening and sugar; add egg and vanilla and beat thoroughly. Fold in flour, mixing well. Pinch off dough and form into one inch in size balls. (A little flour on your fingers will keep the dough from sticking)

Place dough balls on cookie sheet two inches apart. Press dough lightly with a fork to flatten. Sprinkle with sugar. Bake on center rack in the oven 12 minutes or until brown around the edges.

Cool slightly before removing from the pan.
Yield: One dozen, special, delicious cookies.